FROM BLACK AND WHITE TO TECHNICOLOUR

Transforming Limitations Into Brighter Possibilities

KIM LOUISE MORRISON

From Black and White to Technicolour

Copyright © 2015 Kim Louise Morrison

Edited by Juna Guetter

All rights reserved.

ISBN: 1502951460
ISBN-13:978-1502951465

DEDICATION

I wrote this book for *me*. I also wrote this book for *you*. If you are reading this, I wrote it for you. Yes, you. You, who have always wondered if there was a different possibility with feeling stuck in your life, stuck with anger, or a sense of hopelessness that life isn't a whole lot of fun and there isn't much you can do about it. What if there is something you can do about it?

There is a whole world of different and brighter possibilities for you if you'll just make a demand on yourself to find the tools, techniques and information that will work for *you*. You are the only one who can find out what those are for you and what will work for you.

This is my story of how my life went from Black and White to Technicolour. My story of how I found what works for me. I'm sharing it in the fervent hope that you will be inspired to find *your* brighter possibilities. I found mine and so can you.

CONTENTS

1.	It's All About Me..	10
2.	What I Learned From My Romantic Relationships.	16
3.	Awareness of Other Possibilities.....................	36
4.	A Different Possibility for Functioning and Being in the World: Stopping the Mind Chatter............	41
5.	Changing People and Relationships Without Even Trying...	47
6.	A Different Possibility with Work...................	53
7.	A Different Possibility with Receiving...............	61
8.	A Different Possibility with Having, Creating and Receiving Money.................................	66
9.	A Different Possibility with My Body...............	73
10.	It's Not Broken! A Different Possibility with Self-Judgment.........	77
11.	Creating Different Possibilities with Gratitude......	83
12.	CH-CH-Changes...	89

EXPRESSIONS OF GRATITUDE

For my Mom and my brother, Grant, for always being there for me, not just for the good stuff but for when life was rocky. You always had my back and an ear for me.

For Dave, for your love and patience when I spent many hours writing rather than spending time with you. And for listening to me talk incessantly about the book while it was being created.

For Gary Douglas and Dr. Dain Heer, the Founder and Co-creator of Access Consciousness®. Thank you, thank you times a godzilion for this amazing body of work that I and thousands of others have used to create dynamic change in our lives and in the world.

For Juna and Sabine, without whom I may not have found Access and the tools I utilize to transform my life. And for your countless hours of teaching and coaching and kicking my butt when required.

For George Carroll, for providing the platform for me to get off my duff to write this book. Your inspiration has been huge my brother from another mother.

For the crazy, wonderful, sisters and brothers from other mothers who I share the tools, information and body processes of Access Consciousness®. For Jean and Juna for helping with the editing. For Trina and Lisa for helping keep me on track with my writing.

For the many other people who I haven't mentioned personally, who have played a part in supporting me on this journey. Hopefully I have been able to thank you in person.

INTRODUCTION

When I started writing this I had no idea what it was going to look like. I just knew I had to start somewhere. I knew that where I was now was totally different than where I was just six years ago. *Totally different.* And somewhere in that journey was a message I wanted to share with the world.

I knew that if I could somehow share my story to let others know that life doesn't have to be hard. It doesn't have to be all struggle and sacrifice and doing what you think others expect of you and that you never look after you and you never get to be happy. Life doesn't have to suck. If I could get that message across to just *one* person and that it was a contribution to that *one* person, then it was worth it – worth the effort and the fear of rejection and the fear that for some stupid reason that those I love would ridicule me or reject me for what I'm sharing with you.

I also got that I needed to write this for ME. Whether anyone else could receive my message or not.

My life has changed so dramatically and *I* have changed so dramatically in the last six years. I knew I had to share my story so that anyone who is in a place similar to the one that I was in can know that they too can change the things that aren't working in their life.

Does that mean that my life is perfect now? No. Does that mean I've become rich and famous? Well, no, at least not yet…and frankly I don't think I really care if I become rich and famous. I don't believe that's ever been a target of mine. I want to share my story for one simple reason. Because I'm HAPPY! Yup, HAPPY, exactly where I am, right now.

And, I know that this is possible for YOU too…if you'll just choose it and make a demand of yourself to do whatever it takes to get to where you'd like to be. And, where you think you would like to be at the beginning of the journey may change along the way. When you get that there is no physical "there" to get to that will make you happy. There is just YOU. The real YOU inside of you that you need to get to.

I spent most of my adult life until about six years ago in total judgment of me wanting more out of life, wanting something different than what everyone else had. I don't mean in terms of money. I wanted adventure. I wanted constant change. I wanted a different life entirely. I wanted to like myself and I wanted to be *happy*. That was the big one for me. I just wanted to be happy. But, I didn't know how.

I took me a long time to realize that happiness didn't come from outside of me. It came from within. And it was really difficult to be happy when I spent all my time in judgment of me. I had gotten everything in life wrong so far. When was I going to get it right? The right relationship, the right job, the right house, the right friends, the right *life*.

All of these things were external factors so as long as I was sitting in judgment of *me*, there wasn't going to be much of a chance that I was going to be happy.

What changed?

From Black and White to Technicolour

I started a process of self-discovery, of learning, of exploration, of finding the tools, techniques and information I could use to change any and all areas of my life that weren't working for me.

The first real eye opener for me was when I watched the documentary, "The Secret." After that there was Louise Hay, Dr. Wayne Dyer, Anthony Robbins and a myriad of other teachers, books, information and different forms of teachings presented themselves to me. I know now that I had been searching for different teachers all my life. Many have a similar message, "thoughts become things", "your point of view creates your reality", "what you think about you create."

I'm going to fast forward a bit, to now, and let you know that my life on the outside hasn't changed all that drastically. I still live in the same city as I did six years ago, I live in the same house, I have many of the same long-time friends as I had before. I do have a different and amazing partner now. I work at the same company but have a very different position that I actually *enjoy* which I created using the tools I have learned. I do have some wonderful new friends too that I've met from doing the new "modalities" that I practice.

My life now is more joyful, more expansive, more interesting, more varied, more *everything*! And, the most amazing thing of all? I am HAPPY! I'm happy with me (most of the time)...okay, I'm not perfect, yet. I still go into self-judgment, but I am so much aware of when I'm doing that than I used to be. I'm more peaceful, more in allowance of everything around me and in the world that I used to judge as bad and wrong. I'm calmer and I'm more present. I see the glass as damned near full to overflowing now rather than half empty. My life keeps getting better and better and I know, just *know* that there are no limits to what I can create and receive when I choose it.

And, I'm still figuring it out as I go and I'm enjoying the ride. How does it get any better than that!®

My transformation, for the largest part, is thanks to using the tools of this incredibly simple, totally dynamic body of work called Access Consciousness®. So this book and my transformation comes with a HUGE shout of gratitude to the founder of Access Consciousness®, Gary Douglas and his co-creator, Dr. Dain Heer. When I think about how grateful I am for these two magnificent creators who I have the joy of being on planet earth with at the same time, tears of gratitude well up and spill over.

I didn't set out to write a book about Access Consciousness® but it is so front and centre in how and why I have created a life where I am happy almost all of the time and so pivotal to my getting rid of all the crap that wasn't working for me, it may just turn out that there's going to be a whole lot about about Access Consciousness® in the pages that follow.

So, what are all these wonderful and life transforming changes that have occurred in my life that are so magnificent that I need to share them with the world?

Well, I guess I need to give you a bit of my background story first. So here goes...

> *"When I was 5 years old, my mother always told me that happiness was the key to life. When I went to school, they asked me what I wanted to be when I grew up. I wrote down 'happy'. They told me I didn't understand the assignment, and I told them they didn't understand life."* –John Lennon

CHAPTER 1

IT'S ALL ABOUT ME

I spent the better part of my life (at least starting at about age 12 onward) feeling like life was really crappy and I was angry a lot of the time. Oftentimes when our lives are not going as smoothly as we'd like we tend to blame external circumstances, especially our parents. Or is that just me who does that? Well I decided quite early on that my parents were to blame for my inherent unhappiness and for anything that went wrong in my life. They were quite strict and in my young world that meant they were *mean*.

To the best of my recollection, I think I led a reasonably normal early childhood...whatever that means. I had two parents, a brother who was two years older (and I worshiped the very ground my brother walked on since the day I was born and I probably still do, but don't tell him, he'll get a swelled head.) We lived in a nice middle class house in a middle class neighbourhood. My Dad worked at the City waterworks department and my Mom stayed home to raise the two kids and made everything homemade. My Dad got cancer when I was six (brain tumor) and within four months of being diagnosed he decided to head on up to the spirit in the sky. That left my Mom with two very rambunctious kids, a six year old girl (moi) and my eight year old brother. I was a rather precocious kid and I was talking *all the time*, constantly asking questions, bugging my brother every chance I got and always had to be doing *something* other than being quiet.

I have no idea how my Mom dealt with all of that, but I guess it's like many things that life throws at you. If you knew about it ahead of time you would think, "there's no way I can deal with that." But, of course we generally don't know when stuff like that is going to happen. My Mom certainly didn't know when she married my Dad that he wasn't going to be hanging around on earth as long as she might have liked.

So she dealt with being a young widowed mother as best she could. I remember asking her not too long ago, how she dealt with it and how it must have been hard for her to deal with her grief with two little kids to raise. I remember she told me that she was really angry at my Dad for dying and leaving her with two little kids to raise on her own. That actually makes a lot of sense to me now and seems like a pretty normal reaction. Of course she was pissed at him. With the overwhelm of raising two young children alone, she wouldn't have had time to grieve. Nice going Dad.

My Mom met my step-dad sometime during my eighth year and got re-married and we all lived very happily ever after (not). I thought my new 'Dad' was pretty cool for the first few years. That is, until I was about 12 years old. I was all grown up and in Grade 7 and I was talking to a friend in his presence (first mistake) about going to the Grade 7-8 dance at school. Well my step-dad put the kibosh on that right smartly. No 12 year old "daughter" of his was going to a dance with evil boys, not at that age. That was the beginning of a seven year (mostly internal) battle with my step-dad. Only very occasionally was this inner turmoil shown outwardly toward him. My step-dad had been brought up in a very strict household and that was all he knew. He certainly wasn't going to let any daughter of his get eaten up by the hungry sharks out there in the big, bad world. There was no dating, no make-up, very little freedom of speech, unless you agreed with his point of view. He had a lot of strange thoughts and ideas about how to raise kids, and more particularly, how to raise daughters. He pretty much left my brother alone.

I know now that he did the best he could with the tools he had at the time. During that time, however, I would have very gladly thrown him under any passing bus that might have come along. I felt very trapped living under his roof and was angry and frustrated most of the time. I couldn't wait to get out from under his control.

I know my poor Mom was caught in the middle during my teen years with my step-dad being very controlling and also being the main breadwinner in the household. With my mom's generation, it was still often the man and the main breadwinner who made the rules in a household. I would get so angry at her for not intervening and overruling the decisions he made where I was concerned. I would tell her that she was my mother and he *wasn't* my father so why wouldn't she intervene?

I think she just wanted peace in the house and it was easier to deal with a surly teenage daughter that an angry, controlling husband. Not that my Mom wasn't a strong personality herself. I think she just found it easier to go along with whatever decisions my step-dad made to keep the peace with him. My Mom was pretty strict too so she often supported my step-dad's decisions and likely figured it was better off if I wasn't out there getting into all the trouble that teenagers like to get into.

Not that I didn't manage to still get into a bit of trouble, but I kept most of it under wraps.

A lot of the time I didn't even bother to ask my step-dad when I wanted to go out and do things with my friends because it was like pulling teeth and honestly, the anxiety I would suffer leading up to even asking him permission to do something as simple as attending a high school dance was so debilitating for me that I often didn't even bother. I'd sweat and stress about it all week before a Friday night dance and not even get up the nerve to ask because he'd act as if I'd just asked if it was okay to go out and and have sex with 10 boys on the street in front of all the neighbours. By the time Friday evening would roll around, I wouldn't have gotten up the nerve to ask him. I would be so angry and full of hate towards him and I now realize it was towards me too. I'd feel like such a coward for not even asking because, occasionally, he would actually say yes. I'd have all this negative self-talk going through my head like, "he's not going to let me go anyway so why bother asking."

Whenever he did allow me to go out somewhere with friends, there was always the third degree. Who's going to be there? How are you getting there? We lived in the "boonies" so I always needed a ride into town. If it was a house party I wasn't allowed to go unless there was a parent home...and on it went. To be fair a lot of the teenage social events in semi-rural, Midwestern Ontario in the early to mid 1980s involved alcohol so my parents were always concerned about drinking and driving. Drinking was just part of what we did then as teenagers whether it was house parties, a high school dance or even a "gravel run" (hopping into a car with a bunch of friends, some alcohol, and driving the back roads in a rural community). Sometimes we were smart enough to have the driver be sober or at least drink less than the rest of us . Hey, I'm not saying we were all that bright.

Most of my friends did not do drugs (other than alcohol). I did try marijuana, black hash and popped a few beans but luckily I never really took to any of it and I never had any interest in trying harder drugs. Oh, and I *did* inhale.

As much as my step-dad tried to control me and keep me under his thumb while I still lived at home, he also taught me some things that were rather empowering. When I was 12 years old, my step-dad landed a job in a small city a few hours north of where we had been living. We bought a house that was a 10 minute walk from northern Lake Huron in a tourist community with a permanent population of about 2,000 people. Given that we lived in a rural area, life was much different that what it was from living in town. We lived in a bungalow that was surrounded by trees and sometimes a tree or two needed to be taken down. I really can't remember why now. When I was 15 years old my step-dad taught me how to use a chainsaw. Who the hell teaches a 15 year old girl to use a chainsaw?! Well my step-dad taught me. And, I actually didn't mind learning this. He also taught me the proper mix of gasoline to oil in a lawnmower (back in the day when you had to mix them) as I frequently did the grass cutting.

He also taught me how to swing an ax so I could help with the wood chopping for our wood stove. He taught me how to operate the snow-blower so I could clear the driveway when he wasn't home. He even taught me how to shoot a .22 caliber rifle. After getting off the school bus one afternoon I found a raccoon "napping" in our driveway that had died from rabies (or maybe, given all the dried foam around his mouth, he had used that really foamy kind of toothpaste and died from fluoride ingestion - who knows?). Dear old step-dad taught me how to shoot the .22 caliber rifle in case another rabid animal came around when he wasn't home. My Mom sure as heck wasn't going to learn to shoot a gun. I never actually needed to use it but I guess it could have come in handy. If I wasn't enough of a tomboy already, this sure didn't help make me any more feminine.

After I left home at age 19 to attend college I rarely kept in touch as I felt like I had been let out of jail. Free at last, free at last! After I had been on my own for a couple of years I was able to have a fairly good relationship with my step-dad as he was no longer able to control what I did and I was no longer so full of hate and resentment towards him.

His attitude towards me had totally changed. He no longer attempted to control me. Shortly after I had left home he was diagnosed with Parkinson's Disease and I think living with the symptoms of that ailment gave him a whole new perspective on life.

I took a girlfriend "home" to my parents' house for the weekend when I was in my late twenties so we could spend time at the beach. After that weekend my girlfriend said to me, "Your dad is so nice. He's like a big teddy bear."

I hadn't acknowledged up to that point how much he really had changed. I began to see him differently after that. To hold onto any trace of the hate I had towards him in my teens was no longer serving me. It was time to let it go.

I also never realized what a contribution my step-dad was to my life. He did the best job he knew how to do, with the parenting tools that he had available to him.

I was truly sad when he passed away over eight years ago. He had battled a long time with Parkinson's, Type II Diabetes, heart disease, and ultimately, dementia.

> *"Darkness cannot drive out darkness; only light can do that. Hate cannot drive out hate; only love can do that."*
> - Martin Luther King, Jr.

CHAPTER 2

WHAT I LEARNED FROM MY ROMANTIC RELATIONSHIPS

My first "real" boyfriend was a guy I dated in college. He was a year ahead of me in the same Television Broadcasting program. I had no idea how to be in a romantic relationship so I let him take the lead, for the most part. Given my step-dad's strangle hold on my social activities in high school, I had almost no dating experience and no real relationship savvy at all. This guy was actually a lot of fun and we partied a lot as young people will do in college. I knew fairly early on in the relationship that I did not want to spend the rest of my life with this person. He felt differently so I hung in there for some reason. I didn't want to hurt his feelings after all. Nice girls didn't do that. After dating for about a year, he graduated and moved to another city. I knew I really had to get out of the relationship, because as nice as he was (and he really was a great guy), he just wasn't the guy for me.

Suffice it to say, that relationship didn't end well. I chose to have a drunken party fling with an "older man" in my class (okay he was about 30 years old, and when you're 20 years old, that *is* an "older man") and the next weekend when my boyfriend was in town, I did the "honourable" thing and fessed up and ended our romance. All's well that ends well? Not so much. All is not so nice that ends badly. I had done the thing that I despised seeing others doing to their partners. I did reveal my dishonourable behaviour as soon as we saw each other again. It did not end well and there was a long period of us hashing out the ramifications of my actions. In truth, even though it was not a pre-planned course of action, I was thoroughly relieved to be single again.

He had planned out our lives for us, our careers, that we would get married, the whole fairy tale. To me, getting married, settling down, and God forbid, having a family was my idea of a total nightmare, not a fairy tale. I wanted to be free and to have fun and I had decided long ago that that equated to no marriage and no kids. Poor guy. He deserved better. And, last I heard, which is years ago now, he was happily married and a father.

For the next six months or so I had myself a good time being a free-wheeling single girl.

My second partner was another guy from my college class and a single dad. We almost fell into dating without really even trying. We hung out in the same crowd and after graduation he came along and let me know he wanted to do more than just "hang out." I liked him because he was different than any other guys I knew. He didn't make lifelong plans for us and he seemed totally happy to let me be me and do my own thing. He too wanted to be able to do his own thing and not be tied at the hip. By that I don't mean that we saw other people or had an "open" relationship. We were simply both very independent sorts. If I wanted to go socializing and he wanted to stay home and watch the game, we were good with that. The fact that he had a two and half year old son was not what I would have chosen in a partner, but his little boy was absolutely adorable and won me over quite quickly.

Well, that "dating" relationship lasted fifteen years. Likely about ten years longer than the shelf life on the label. Our "doing our own thing" worked out for a while but at some point I know I realized that we really didn't have a relationship that was honouring each other so much as a cohabitation that was convenient.

The real "fun" started after we'd been together about ten years and my partner's son, who was 12 years old by this time, was coming to live with us. I quit my job and we left the big city and moved to a much smaller town close to where my partner's parents lived and close to where the son had lived with his mother up to that point. At that time my partner was doing freelance work in television and traveling a lot. In my typical bossy manner I told him that under no circumstances was I going to be the "main parent" for his son. I did not want to give up my come and go as I pleased lifestyle. He was the father and he needed to be around so he better quit freelancing and get a "normal" job so that he could be home to raise his son. I didn't actually notice that he stood there silent to my ultimatum.

After our big move to the small town and settling into family life, it became apparent to me that being a step-mom with my partner who was rarely home was going to be hard work. There were a lot of unresolved issues that I was definitely not equipped to handle. It also became apparent that my partner was *not* going to cease his lucrative freelance career. When I reminded him after several months of my provision that he get a "normal" job so that he was home to actually raise *his* son and not leaving me to do it by myself, his simple response was that he had never agreed to stop freelancing, simply because it was what I wanted.

The next five years were not exactly joyful for any of us. My stepson and I actually had a pretty good relationship. There were definitely some rocky times and my bitterness over my partner never being around during those times grew and our time together when he was home became less and less amicable as time went on. I know

now that I really could have used so many of the tools that I learned later to cope with many of the situations that arose during that time.

What is it in us that makes us stay in relationships long after they have run their course? I know during the times that I was raising my step-son I often thought, "well if I leave, who's going to look after him?"

We often take on these roles in life and then take ownership of a particular situation such that we feel that we are entirely responsible. This seems true even if it's something we have merely decided is true and it's not actually the way things are. I had decided that my partner's son was my responsibility. I would look like a bad person if I left and there wouldn't be anyone to look after him if I left.

When I did leave that relationship, my partner's son ended up leaving at the same time. He was 17 years old by then, no longer in school, and was headed out on his own path of discovery. Sometimes we are so caught up in a situation that when we are in the middle of it we can't see it clearly until we remove ourselves and can look back on it. Then we realize how significant we make things and how much trauma and drama we attach to our perceived outcome.

Six months after that relationship ended (are you seeing the six month thing here?) I met my husband, Dann. We fell in love very quickly. I think the "L" word (no not *that* "L" word, the word L-O-V-E) was expressed within three weeks of our first date.

I remember seeing an aunt not long after Dann and I started dating and she asked me about this new man I was seeing and I gave her a huge smile and said I was "smitten". And, I was, thoroughly head over heels in love. For the first time and it was almost overwhelming.

From Black and White to Technicolour

No offence to my previous partner. I did love him, but I realized that I had loved him more like a buddy that I'd had a sexual relationship with. Not the kind of love that you have for someone you want to spend your life with. I had also thought that how much I loved my previous partner was as much as I was actually capable of loving someone.

I knew that gaga, head over heels love *existed*. I just didn't think that it would ever exist for *me* or that I could love anyone that much because I'd never experienced it. I knew I had a lot of internal anger and resentment built up in me and thought that I wasn't capable of the kind of love you see in romantic movies.

When my husband and I met we had so many connection points. I had taken Television Broadcasting in college. He had taken Audio Visual Technician. We had both been skydiving. We both loved chocolate. His middle name was Alexander, which was also the middle name of both my father and my brother. We had both lost a parent at a young age (my dad when I was age six and his mother died when he was eighteen). We both loved running and working out. We both loved camping and the outdoors. We had both been brought up in very strict households. I think we found each other at a time when we were really looking for someone to love and for someone to love us back. We fell in love with being in love.

We did sweet and considerate things for each other. He would surprise me with silly gifts like big puffy slippers in the shape of puppies. He fixed things around my house. A month before he moved in with me he climbed up into my attic and plugged all the holes in the roof that were leaking rain into the house during a torrential downpour. Having a sprinkler system coming through my dining room chandelier was not my idea of a fun time.

He surprised me by installing ceiling fans in several rooms because we didn't have air conditioning at the time. He tore down two falling apart sheds in my back yard and built a new one. He did all sorts of handyman things that my previous partner had never done. They were the kinds of things that I thought a partner should do, that I didn't know how to do and I was so grateful for him being my knight in shining armor.

As much as I prided myself on being an independent woman and one who didn't *need* a man for anything (well, maybe one thing, wink, wink), I revelled in having someone do such wonderful things for me. He told me I deserved to have someone treat me this way. I thought, who was I to deserve having a man treat me so well?!

Several of my friends were jealous of me and told me so. They thought he was such a great catch and wished their men treated them as well as mine did. One of them would even point out to her husband all the things that Dann did for me and why didn't he do those sorts of things for her?

Dann also had an awesome sense of humour. I loved that about him and many other people did too. He took to my family right away and they to him.

I did the "woman" stuff in the house and he did the "man" stuff. I was a good cook and he was very handy. We were inseparable and couldn't stand to be away from each, not for even a night or we missed each other terribly. I know now that we were in love with being in love. Don't get me wrong, we actually did love each other. I know that we also chose to not see in the other person the things that didn't work for us or the things that would later help to create a rift in our relationship.

Very early in our romance he let me know about the skeletons in his closet. He told me about his past legal trouble, his bankruptcy and his depression issues. He was very forthright about it all and he wanted to give me an "out" before we got too serious. It was already too late for me. I loved him. I appreciated his honesty and I knew that now that he was with me and we were so happy and so in love that none of the past would matter.

I did notice that during the "reveal" process, that every time he opened another can of worms, there was always the tale of someone who had wronged him, or who caused a certain behaviour in him. There were outside circumstances that weren't his fault for the misdeed that had occurred. There was never any ownership on his part for the black marks in his history book.

We started dating in May, moved in together after about six months and within nine months we got engaged in December. We planned to marry the following August.

Near the end of the following June, two months before we were to be married, Dann experienced a workplace injury that caused herniation in several discs in his lower back. That was the beginning of a long and painful journey for him.

We got married in August as planned. It was a small ceremony with about 40 people in attendance. We had the reception in our back yard under a canopy. It was a fairy tale day for me.

We went camping for our honeymoon as that was about all that we could afford. We didn't get too adventurous with the outdoor activities due to Dann's back injury.

During this time and for a long time after his injury, Dann was taking a fair amount of pain medication. The more time that elapsed after his injury and the longer it took for his back to heal, the more unhappy he became. He started seeing a family doctor who was also a therapist and he was taking two to three different antidepressants at any given time.

After some time had passed, he started getting angry with his constant state of being in pain. He made me the target of some of his angry outbursts. I have always avoided conflict so rather than standing up for myself, I would simply clam up and internally justify any nasty behaviour as the pain talking or his depression talking or some other excuse.

It's funny to me that many people have the point of view that people don't change. Where Dann was concerned, this is not true. He really did change. I even remember the instant when I physically felt sick in my gut as I saw him change before my eyes.

He was angry about something. I don't even recall what the particular trigger was now but it had to do with this constant state of pain. I was standing in the kitchen and he came in and was spewing and venting about what I believe was some wrong that had been done to him. This was just after the orthopaedic surgeon told him that he was not a candidate for back surgery. He had pinned all of his hopes for recovery on having back surgery to relieve the pain of his herniated discs. Unfortunately his most recent MRI at that time had shown that his discs were not as herniated as they had been previously. His pain had increased however due to the fact that he had a pinched nerve between two of the discs.

When he got the news that there would be no surgery, it really set him off.

So, back to the kitchen incident. Dann came into the kitchen and stopped while he was on his rant and looked at me and his face was so full of rage and pain and despair. It was like nothing I had ever seen before. He said something about being so angry that he wanted to hit something and he glared at me as if I was his mortal enemy. In that instant I felt a part of me leave and just take a hike from my being. I don't recall ever being present to that kind of intensely hateful and hurtful emotion before or since that day.

I looked at him and said that he was looking at me as if he hated *me* and wanted to hit *me* even though I wasn't the person he was angry with in that moment. He said that he wished I could feel the pain that he lived with for just one day so that I would know what it was like. I was so stunned by his palpable rage that I just stood there dumbfounded and didn't say anything else.

He proceeded to go down to the basement and smash and break things. He never did hit me, not that day or any other.

After that incident, he never went back to being the person I thought I knew or the person I had fallen in love with. His wonderful sense of humour was gone. And all those really sweet things that he did for me stopped. And he was never kind to himself again after that time either. Maybe he never had been all that kind to himself.

He had a few jobs after he was deemed well enough to be off worker's compensation insurance but they were all call centre jobs or jobs that weren't suitable for him.

Every new job he got didn't last long and there was always someone who was treating him badly or some sort of problem that made him leave the job.

He finally landed a job working as a manager at a storage facility. He actually quite liked that job and the money was better than the call centre jobs. I was quite relieved too as oftentimes the two of us had been living on my one pay cheque so there was also a financial burden that always hung between us and he hated that I was supporting us both and he didn't feel like he was much of a contribution in that way.

After he had been at the storage facility job for about a month I thought, "man this is great, he can start helping out with the household expenses."

Well, Dann's favourite hobby, and occasionally even one that earned a bit of money was photography. So after he had brought home a pay cheque or two on this new job, he got on the computer one evening and announced he was so happy that he was able to order this very fancy and quite expensive new lens that he had had his eye on for a while. Wasn't that great? Hell no, it isn't great, I thought. How about helping me with the household bills? I was really pissed off internally but I never said a thing to him as I didn't want to make him angry.

I never really noticed that after he "changed" I watched what I said around him. I didn't have my friends come over anymore as he couldn't handle trying to be social or worse yet, he hated it when they fussed over him because of his back pain and when they would ask him how he was. He said he hated their pity.

The funny thing is, about a year later, a friend said to me that Dann sure liked to feel sorry for himself. I didn't really see it at the time, but I did later on.

During this time Dann would frequently mention that it was no good for me to have him around in the state that he was in. He really wanted to be by himself most of the time and wasn't up to having to try to put on a happy face for me or to even communicate with me. He mentioned a few times that he was thinking about leaving so that he could be by himself and he didn't have to worry about treating me badly.

A lot of the time he didn't even bother trying to communicate with me. Our physical relationship became non existent.

During all this time he was also drinking steadily to add his own pain "medication" to all the prescription medication that he was already taking.

At the end of a particular Sunday he had had quite a few alcoholic beverages even though he almost never showed any outward signs of intoxication. I realized after I had cleaned up the supper dishes that he had gone outside and moved my car from the driveway onto the street. I went out to the front of the house as he was walking back to the driveway, heading towards his car and I asked him what he was doing. I knew he had had quite a lot to drink and I didn't want him driving.

He said he was going out for a drive in his car and he was going to crash his car and kill himself. I snatched his keys out of his hand and said there was no way I was letting him drive and what if he killed someone else in the process and he certainly wasn't going to kill himself if I had any say in the matter.

He then proceeded to walk off down the street, with me in tow. I of course was frantic wondering what he was going to do next. I had no idea what he was going to do but letting him kill himself was not on my agenda for that particular Sunday evening. I don't recall exactly what he said while we walked down the street but I do remember it was rather heated and I know he was advising me that what he wanted to do was not my business and I should stay out of it.

I remember walking back to the house together at some point and at the front door just before we were about to enter the house he looked at me and said "fuck you" with about as much hate and anguish in his eyes as I'd ever seen. I remember being rather surprised at that and thinking, wow, he really *does* hate me now.

He might have hated me in that moment for I had foiled his plans to end his suffering that evening. After we went in the house we just sat down in our living room and talked for a bit and I think the wind left his sails for we went to bed almost as if nothing had happened. He promised not to harm himself. We both got up and went to work the next morning. It was all a bit surreal.

I remember thinking that I didn't know what I was supposed to do after we went back in the house. I thought about calling the police to ask them to take him to the hospital and have him on suicide watch, but I didn't. Some part of me wanted to pretend that that incident had never happened and calling the police would have made it all too real. There was a rather bizarre aspect to the whole evening anyway. Part of me kept thinking that it wasn't really happening. It was all some kind of bad, crazy dream. This kind of thing might happen to other people, but not to me.

I don't think it was long after that incident that Dann told me that he had decided that he was going to move out and he had already found an apartment. I asked him when and he said it would be in two weeks. I told him that that wasn't a lot of warning. I was a bit stunned. I think he was looking for some theatrics or tears from me or expected me to beg him not to go. I was numb by then. He looked at me and said, "Well, aren't you going to say anything?" I responded that there wasn't much to say. He had obviously made up his mind and he'd already signed the lease for his new apartment.

He moved out at the beginning of June. I remember that it was a Wednesday and I took that day off work. I got up in the morning and went to the gym so that I wouldn't be home when the movers arrived. I didn't want to be around for that. When I got home, all of his stuff was gone except for his cat. He had wanted me to keep the cat and I refused. She was his cat and she was 19 years old. I said it was enough for me to deal with him leaving, I wasn't going to deal with the inevitable passing of his cat too.

After he made the decision to leave, it wasn't like anything really changed all that much more for us. I have described a few incidents where he wasn't very nice to me and there were more, but for the most part, we had been living like two roommates who actually got along quite well most of the time. He hadn't been communicating with me that much over the past year. He spent most of his time at home watching TV. He had long ago stopped going to family functions and he didn't have any friends left. When he moved out, it was really quite amicable.

We had been married for just less than four years so it was quite easy to divvy up the household items. We basically each kept whatever we had brought into the relationship and everything else was divided according to who was most likely to use it. There was no fighting or squabbling over anything. In fact, I remember that I bought him a house warming gift for his new apartment.

We stayed in almost daily communication after he first moved out and he kept his key to the house. He was quite "tech savvy" and if I needed help with my computer or some such thing he simply came over to the house while I was at work and let himself in to do whatever it was I needed help with. We also would get together for dinner at either of our homes every couple of weeks at first. This dwindled to once a month after a time.

As time went on our communication became slightly less frequent but we were still what you would call quite chummy. We were like old friends who had once been more than that. You could tell that he was so much more at ease living on his own and he told me so on several occasions. He's also lamented how I was much better off with him not living with me as he knew that he had not treated me very well for quite a while.

I also realized very quickly how I had been walking on eggshells around him the last couple of years and I really hadn't let me be me around him. I realized I had always been on guard in case something upset him.

I still cared for him but I no longer loved him like I used to because he was no longer the man I had fallen in love with and married. That man was long gone. His joy was gone and so was his humour. His affect was very flat. His personality had changed.

About a year or so after he left, we got a joint divorce. All done with total civility. Within a year and a half of him leaving he was fired from his job. I believe he started to have some issues with his employer when he wasn't able to hold his anger in check. He re-injured his back a few months later when he slipped on some ice outside his apartment building. Shortly after that he met a woman whom he fell in love with very quickly. She unfortunately didn't get the benefit of knowing the man I fell in love with; however, she still saw the good person he was and he could still be very loving when he wanted to be.

It was funny. He didn't want to tell me that he had a girlfriend. I found out because she called me one day after getting my number off his cell phone. She wanted help in dealing with what she believed were suicidal tendencies on his part. Things were going downhill for him again.

During the next three or four months Dann and I only saw each other about once a month. Sometimes I wonder why we maintained our friendship but I guess neither of us ever let go completely.

The last time I saw him, he came over to my house for dinner and we sat out on my back deck and other than having a reasonably good relationship with his girlfriend, things really weren't going very well for him. He said his pain was very bad, he didn't see that he would ever live with his girlfriend as he was too volatile. He was applying for disability insurance because his doctor didn't think he was capable of working anymore and unbeknownst to me, he was declaring bankruptcy (again).

Two weeks later I got an email one evening from him that he had sent to a small group of people which read, "So long and thanks for all the fish." Yes, a rather strange email. It's a quote from the fourth book in the series, "The Hitchhiker's Guide to the Galaxy." According to Wikipedia, science fiction fans use it as a humorous way to say goodbye.

Dann had sent a similar email out to a bunch of friends the night that he was planning to go out and crash his car and kill himself.

So when I got this email, about two hours after he sent it, I called him right away to see if he was okay. He didn't answer. I knew that he and his girlfriend had planned a camping trip with some friends the previous weekend so I called her to see if everything was okay. I left her a couple of messages but received no response. I thought that maybe they had broken up or had a fight. He had commented on our last visit that he was worried that he was treating her like he had treated me after he became "sick."

I attempted to check in with my inner knowing to see if he was okay and I got that he was. And, he likely was by that time but in a different manner of being "okay" than what most people perceive being okay as.

The second day I called him a couple more times with no response to my messages and I continued to call his girlfriend as well. Her voice mail was now full.

I decided to call his landlord to see if there was any way they could check on him. They wouldn't do anything without the police. I called the police and asked them to go and check on him. They were rather hesitant at first given that I was his ex-wife and they didn't understand the email reference so I had to do a little convincing and explain his history of depression. They called me again when they reached the apartment building to re-confirm all the information and said they would call me back within 20 minutes.

They didn't call me back.

An hour and a half later, the receptionist at my office called and advised that there were two police officers there to see me. I knew that this was not a good sign.

From Black and White to Technicolour

I went into a boardroom with the two officers and they had the rather shitty job of telling me that they had found my ex-husband in his apartment and that he was no longer living. I'm assuming those two must have drawn the short straws that day. Not a job I would wish on anyone. I think I was in shock for a second or two and then I started to cry. I think a part of me knew before the police arrived that he had taken his life and another part of me didn't believe it. It was all so unreal. I was on autopilot for the rest of that day and likely for some time after.

I called my boyfriend and asked him to come down and sit with me while I gave the police officers a statement. I really needed someone to be with me and I am very grateful for the man who was my boyfriend at that time and who I'm happy to still call a friend.

Dann didn't really have family to speak of. Both of his parents were gone and he had a sister who he was estranged from - his choice. I took on the job of "cleaning up" Dann's affairs.

Dann had not wanted a funeral so two months after he passed, his girlfriend, a few of my friends and family members (which included my mother and brother) and a few of his friends, took Dann's ashes to a conservation area that he loved and we did a small private, personal service and scattered his ashes.

I stayed angry with Dann for a long time after that. I really wasn't all that pissed off at him for killing himself. No, I was pissed off that he had stopped trying, that he had given up on life, given up on getting better, for blaming everyone else for everything that had ever gone wrong in his life and I was pissed off at him for *changing*.

How dare he come into my life, while being this wonderful, kind, caring, humorous and full of life man who loved me like I was the best thing that had ever happened to him? How dare he do all that and then completely change into someone different? How dare he do that to *me*?!

It took me a long while to learn that no one does anything *to* you. It's how you react that matters. When I was having some facilitation with a wonderful Access Consciousness® facilitator and I was asking for help with letting go, forgiving and to stop being so pissed off at Dann, she gave me a wonderful way of looking at things. She said be grateful for when things were good and be grateful for when things *changed*.

It was a total judgment for me to decide that things went bad. Did they really get bad or did they just change? I know, I know, you may look at my story and say, but they *did get bad!* If that's how I choose to look at it, then I stay in judgment. If I look at it from the perspective that things simply changed then I can be grateful that that is just how it was.

I am grateful now for everything that Dann brought to my life. Like I said before, I had never had anyone love me like he did or do all the kind and loving things that he did and fuss over me and get all mushy with me and treat me like I was someone to be cherished.

I learned some valuable lessons from my favourite ex-husband.

Whether you perceive something as really wonderful or really terrible, keep in mind that it can change.

Never doubt your inner knowing. You know what you know. If your Spidey senses are tingling it's for a reason. There were lots of signs and red flags early on in my relationship with Dann that things were not going to be all sunshine and roses, but I chose to ignore those signs because I was in love. It is hard for me to say now, in hindsight, if I would have changed anything about my relationship with Dann. Would I have still married him if I had taken a closer look and acknowledged my awareness that not everything in his past was the way he described it from his point of view?

I knew he had had depression issues, financial issues and health issues. The Pollyanna in me, decided that it didn't matter because he was different now with me and everything would be great because we were together and we were in love. Love conquers all, right?

If I had asked questions and tapped into my awareness I might have chosen differently. But then again, I might not have.

Another lesson I learned was to never cut yourself off from being who you really are with another person. That doesn't serve you or them. Dann got really tired of me tiptoeing around him and fussing over him when he was sick. Me not choosing to be me, didn't serve either of us and I didn't even realize until after he moved out, how much I had been doing that. I thought he needed me to be ultra sensitive to his needs and to look after him and fuss over him when he was in pain and feeling depressed so I always looked after what he needed first without considering what I needed.

He told me later that my fussing over him drove him nuts. He felt like I was acting more like his nurse and his mother rather than being his wife. I never thought to ask him what he required of me so that I could be whatever that was for him, if whatever that was also worked for me as well.

Before Dann committed suicide, I had always judged suicide as a wrongness when I had heard of other people doing it. How could they do that to their partners, their family, and their friends?! It was the coward's way out!

I don't feel that way anymore. You may totally disagree with me and think I'm cold and insensitive for saying this, but Dann did the only thing he thought he could do to get out of his physical and emotional pain. Who am I to say that it was wrong? I know that he is in a happier place now where he's pain free, physically and emotionally. He is just "being", without a body, and what if that's okay?

Dann, I am grateful for you. Thank you. I know you are "out there" wherever we go in between our physical incarnations, hanging out having a good time and you are no longer in pain. I'll see you again my friend...but not for quite some time.

I have so many things to do here first.

"Forgiveness is not always easy. At times, it feels more painful than the wound we suffered, to forgive the one that inflicted it. And yet, there is no peace without forgiveness."
— Marianne Williamson

CHAPTER 3

AWARENESS OF OTHER POSSIBILITIES

Right around the time that Dann left me, I had my first introduction to this weird and wacky body of work called Access Consciousness®. I was introduced to it by two women whom I had known on more of an acquaintance basis for several years. The one woman, Juna Guetter, I had met more recently by taking Nia fitness classes with her. Juna knew a lot about bodies and how bodies liked to move. After a number of years of doing Access, she has become an even more phenomenal facilitator and healer of people and how they function with and in their bodies.

The other woman, Sabine Hildebrandt, I had been introduced to several years prior by a mutual friend. She was a life coach at that time and did some kind of woo woo stuff that I knew nothing about. I was totally intrigued by her because she was *different* and she had these strange healing capacities that I was totally in awe of. She was different in a way that totally inspired me and opened my eyes to the way she seemed totally at ease with herself. Something that I had never experienced.

I remember the first time I met Sabine. This was several years before she got into Access. I had never met a life coach before. One of my girlfriends had gifted Dann a session with Sabine to help him clear out some "negative" energy that he had been wanting to release (for lack of a better explanation that is too involved to go into here). As soon as Sabine came into our house I was intrigued. She was doing some sort of crystal healing session with Dann and I was so mesmerized I forgot what I would normally have considered good manners and asked if I could watch her do the session with him. I was actually surprised when she said sure, no problem.

During the session she placed crystals around Dann while he lay on the bed. I sat on a dining room chair just inside the doorway to the room, watching and waiting for some miracle to happen. There really wasn't much to physically "see" as the healing was taking place internally.

As Sabine was leaving our house that night she looked at me and said something to the effect of "you have sight. Come and see me sometime if you want to explore that." Some part of me knew then that she was correct and the other, dismissive part of me thought, "who, me? She doesn't know what she's talking about. I don't have any special abilities." I didn't know then that we all have these abilities to varying degrees, we just have to develop them.

Dann continued to see Sabine for some time after that for various healing sessions.

After he injured his back at work and herniated a couple of discs in his back he would go to her for treatments. He came home after one such treatment in total awe. He said when he left her place after his treatment that day he had no pain at all. Zero, zilch, nada, none. It shows how powerful we as beings with bodies are if we simply choose to receive healing and allow our bodies to heal. Well that lasted for several days and then, likely given his mental state, he slowly started to feel the pain again and I don't think he ever got back to that pain free place again.

This made me so very aware of what a strong mechanism our minds are, especially our subconscious minds. Some part of him didn't believe that he could be healed that easily and I also know that some part of him didn't believe that he *deserved* to be healed. He and I had numerous discussions about this.

Around the time that Dann left me, I took a class with Juna and Sabine that was my first introduction to Access. During this class they introduced a different way of looking at money, at life and at me than I had ever seen before. Part of it (the verbal processing) annoyed the hell out of me and parts of it made so much common sense to me that I thought, "wait, I already *know* this stuff, but why haven't I cognitively acknowledged this before?" A lot of Access is about tapping into one's inner knowing and all the places where we've had blinders on previously.

I could see that there was something different possible. That the autopilot way of functioning where I had lived most of my life wasn't the only possibility available.

What I also knew was that both Juna and Sabine seemed a whole lot happier than I had seen them before (and I thought they were happy *before* this). They also had this sense of something greater, something more, an expansiveness to their lives that was very contagious and made me think, "I don't know what you guys are doing but I'll have some of *that*!"

They were teaching that, with Access, you didn't have to re-examine and dissect all the things in your life that weren't working for you and you didn't have to have hours of counselling to release old hurts and triggers from your past. They had never seen any other modality that was this simple and yet so dynamic, and that had such immediate results for changing anything in your life that wasn't working for you. I figured what the heck, it was working so well for them, I was having some of that too!

A couple of months after this I took my first Access Bars® class.

The Bars® is totally experiential and I cannot do it justice by even attempting to explain it here but I'll try to give you an idea. The core of Access Consciousness® which originated roughly 25 years ago is this crazy simple hands-on body process called Access Bars® or simply, "The Bars."

My first experience with The Bars was in August 2009 when I attended an Access Bars class taught by Juna and Sabine and there I had my "Bars run" for the first time. Talk about completely freaking mind blowing and life changing!

The best way I can describe how you feel after a Bars session would be to compare it to the space in your head that you are in just before you go to sleep. You know that place where your mind is totally quiet, you aren't quite asleep yet but you're not awake either? It's something like that, but then again it's not because even though your mind is very quiet, you can often feel totally energized at the same time. Your mind chatter totally slows to a crawl or even stops but you also feel really alive and yet peaceful, all at the same time. You see, I really can't explain it.

Here's the description of the The Bars from the accessconsciousness.com website:

> "The first class in Access is The Bars®. Did you know there are 32 points on your head which, when gently touched, effortlessly and easily release anything that doesn't allow you to receive? These points contain all the thoughts, ideas,

beliefs, emotions, and considerations that you have stored in any lifetime. This is an opportunity for you to let go of everything!

Each Access Bars® session can release 5-10 thousand years of limitations in the area of your life that corresponds with the specific Bar being touched. This is an incredibly nurturing and relaxing process, undoing limitation in all aspects of your life that you are willing to change.

How much of your life do you spend doing rather than receiving? Have you noticed that your life is not yet what you would like it to be? You could have everything you desire (and even greater!) if you are willing to receive lots more and maybe do a little less! Receiving or learning The Bars® will allow this to begin to show up for you.

Access Bars® has assisted thousands of people to change many aspects of their body and their life including sleep, health and weight, money, sex and relationships, anxiety, stress and so much more. At worst you will feel like you have just had a phenomenal massage. ***At best your whole life can change into something greater with total ease.***

I highlighted the last part because I wanted to emphasize that this is what has occurred for me. My whole life *has* changed. It *is* greater and I have way more *ease* in absolutely every area of my life now.

How does it get any better than that?®

CHAPTER 4

A DIFFERENT POSSIBILITY FOR FUNCTIONING AND BEING IN THE WORLD: STOPPING THE MIND CHATTER

I had no idea how much mind chatter I had until I actually experienced the *opposite* of mind chatter. It had always been there so I just assumed that a noisy mind was just part of who I was and how I functioned in the world. My mind was so chatty that for a long time, I inwardly wondered if I had adult ADHD. I would have a million thoughts a second and didn't seem to have the capacity to focus on anything for more than a few seconds. I had also always been told I was too hyper and needed to "calm down."

I would have trouble focusing when I was having a conversation with someone. My mind would have a million other thoughts floating around while I was trying to pay attention to what someone was telling me.

A lot of my mind chatter was also a constant barrage of either self-judgment or what I thought was me judging other people and other things.

There are a couple of wonderful Access tools that I use to drastically reduce my mind chatter. One of them is having my Bars run regularly, which I talked about in the previous chapter. As soon as someone places their hands on my head to start running my Bars, my mind becomes this quiet oasis of expansive space and peace. I had no idea this was even possible!

After a Bars session, it feels like my body and brain have heaved this big sigh of relief. I feel very calm and energized at the same time and my mind is...well, peaceful, quiet and happy. This is so hard to describe in words. It really has to be experienced.

The other amazing Access tool I use to quiet my mind chatter is asking myself the question, "Who Does This Belong to?®" for every thought, feeling and emotion that I have.

According to Gary Douglas, the founder of Access, 98% of our thoughts, feelings and emotions don't actually belong to us. What?!! Yes, that's right, 98%! Yes, I know, it's a bit unbelievable to think that most of the things we think and feel don't even belong to us.

Science has proven that everything is energy and that includes thought forms, feelings and emotions. So if we are all energetic beings and our thoughts and feelings are also waves of energy, wouldn't it make sense that we pick up the energetic waves of those around us *all the time*?

Have you ever noticed that you can be in a pretty good mood and then you come across a person who is sad and after spending a few minutes with that person, that you become sad too? And, whatever it is that they are sad about has nothing to do with you. So is that *your* sadness or *their* sadness?

I love the following example as it's something that happens to me all the time. Have you ever noticed when you've been driving your car and you have all these other cars around you and you are driving along quite happily, singing along with the radio (loudly and off-key...oh wait, that's just me) and all of a sudden you find you are annoyed or angry. No one has cut you off. No one is riding your bumper. What's with that? Is that anger even yours? Well, are you picking up other people's energy? How many of the people in the cars around you are happy?

We are these energetic sponges who go about our lives taking on and picking up other people's energy in the form of thoughts, feelings and emotions. With all of this information coming at us from all directions, it creates a lot of mind chatter. That is, until we have the means to stop it. What if there was an easy way to quiet that monkey mind?

This is a wonderful Access tool for helping you have a whole lot more ease and space in your world. It will create way less mind chatter. So if you like your chatty mind, definitely don't try this.

I know this tool is going to sound a little weird (okay, a whole lot weird). Every time you get a thought, feeling or emotion, just ask "Who Does This Belong to?®" If the feeling that you were experiencing lightens up in any way, it wasn't yours to begin with. So just return that bad boy to sender. What?!! Okay, now I've really gone off the rails, right? Wrong. This tool really works.

Here's *how* it works. When you get a thought or a feeling about something and you ask, "Who Does This Belong to?®" notice how that feels in your body. Generally, you are going to be more aware of the thoughts, feelings and emotions that you deem to be "negative." When you use this tool and ask the question, "Who Does This Belong to?®" you may notice a "lightness" in your body or your being after asking the question. The best way I have to describe it and how this shows up for me is that when I ask "Who Does This Belong to?®", I will usually feel a lightness in my chest. It's different for everyone and you may perceive this in a totally different way. It may not actually be a "physical" sensation for you, but more of a "lightness in your being."

Once you ask the question, "Who Does This Belong To?®" and you feel a "lightness" or a shift in the energy, then that's a clear indication that this thought (or whatever it is) doesn't belong to you.

Say to yourself, "return to sender." Now, you might think, well if I pick up sadness from someone I care about and ask the question, and it lightens up, I don't want to "return" it to them. Well, you aren't. The "return to sender" is acknowledging that this thought, feeling or emotion doesn't belong to you and you are simply returning it to the originating source. Just because you picked up on someone else's thought, feeling or emotion, doesn't mean that you took it *away* from them anyway. They are still experiencing it as well.

You won't necessarily even know cognitively where the thought, feeling or emotion came from. You don't need to know. You may just have an awareness of it by asking the question. If things lighten up in your world using this tool, then my point of view is that it works and you have gotten rid of something that doesn't serve you whether it's sadness, negative thoughts or a physical pain or sensation of some kind.

This works for physical sensations or what we perceive as pain as well. I can't count the number of times that I've had what I perceive as physical pain and when I actually remember to ask, "Who Does This Belong to?®", it lightens up. This really does work. It is so amazing and I'm so tickled when I do this and an ache or pain either lightens up immensely or completely goes away. How does it get any better than that?!®

An absolutely amazing exercise is to ask yourself, "Who Does This Belong to?®" for every thought, feeling and emotion that you have for three days straight. Yes, that means for the *all* thoughts, feelings and emotions you have for those three days. Even the good ones.

When you use this tool for three days straight you will find it totally changes your way of being. I'm going to be totally honest here and admit that it has been a huge stumbling point for me because I'd start this challenge and part way through I'd forget to use the tool. I'd have appointment reminders in my phone to keep me on track, a repeating appointment in my work calendar, sticky notes all over my house and my office to remind myself to ask this question. Naturally, I was also making myself wrong and judging myself for not keeping totally on track with this.

So, if you use this tool and do it for three days straight, give yourself a break if you forget to use it for half an hour, or three hours, or even a whole day. Just get back on track when you remember and use whatever reminder methods work for you.

I can't tell you the number of times I've thought I was angry or sad and I've asked "Who does this belong to?®" and the energy or heaviness in my chest totally shifts. I've caught myself being sad or crying over something and when I actually *remember* to ask 'Who does this belong to?" and the "heavy" feeling dissipates, I am still in awe at how well this works.

The point of the exercise is to just do it. Notice what you notice after doing this for three days. It really does work. You will be amazed at how your mind chatter will slow down.

Dr. Dain Heer has a wonderful YouTube video entitled: "Who Does This Belong To? Dr. Dain Heer & Access Consciousness" from August 11, 2009. I have heard Dr. Dain say, "after three days you'll walk around like you are a walking, talking meditation."

Do you have a lot of mind chatter? I think you'll find that you don't if you choose to give this tool a try for three days.

But then again, what would you possibly want with a quiet mind?

CHAPTER 5

CHANGING PEOPLE AND RELATIONSHIPS WITHOUT EVEN TRYING

I didn't get for a long time that I had a choice in how to "be" in my relationships. Nor did I get that my number one relationship should be with *me*, always. I just thought that my relationships with the people in my life were the way that they were and that was that. Until I had the tools to change all of my relationships for the better.

My relationships with the people around me have changed. Other than the absolute most important relationship of all, my relationship with ME, my next most significant and long standing relationship has been my relationship with my Mom.

My relationship with my Mom has absolutely, definitely gone from black and white to technicolour. I used to feel that every time we either got together or talked on the phone that if I said something was black, she would say that it was white. And, if I said something was white, she'd say it was black. We had that mother-daughter butting heads thing going on a lot and it had always been that way. Things had gotten easier between us the last number of years before I discovered Access, but after I started using the tools and information of Access, our relationship became so much smoother, so much easier and so much more one of mutual respect and friendship.

I have a friend who describes how after her first Bars session she really didn't feel anything and thought that it was a big fat waste of time. Many people feel that way after the first time they have their Bars run because the change that is experienced can be very subtle. This same friend has an adult son whom she butted heads with every time she talked on the phone with him. About three weeks after getting her Bars run for the first time she had a telephone call with her son and after hanging up the phone she realized that it was the easiest conversation that she had ever had with him. When she asked herself if that easy conversation had anything to do with her having her Bars run, she got a huge YES.

How do I explain that? I have no idea. All I know is that this stuff is weird and wacky and it works!

Gary Douglas, the founder of Access has pointed out many times that you will "do the work" of Access and those around you reap the benefits. Pretty cool, huh?

Back to my Mom and me.

I've already told you about how things were with my Mom and I when I was growing up. We never really seemed to see eye to eye and we just weren't that close and that was just the way it was and would always be. Or so I thought.

I cannot give you one particular instance or exact moment where I noticed that our relationship had totally changed. It came to me as an aha moment one day and I realized that we simply didn't argue hardly at all anymore. Do we agree on everything? No. Do we spend a lot more time together than we used to? No. It's that our relationship is so much easier now. Maybe a lot of that is because I have dropped my resistance and reaction to all my Mom's points of view and realized that they are just that. They are her points of view on things and I don't need to fight for my point of view if it's different than hers. Just because she has a point of view on something doesn't mean that she is trying to make my point of view wrong or bad. There is so much more allowance and understanding between us now and for that I am eternally grateful.

A Different Possibility with Romantic Relationships

After what I thought was a great relationship with Dann not turning out so well, I simply decided that I was terrible at romantic relationships. Along with cutting off my awareness with Dann and choosing only to see the "good" things in him and ignoring all the areas where I knew things weren't going to work with us, I also got another really important piece.

My romantic relationships were never going to work until I learned to put *me* first. I had *never* put myself first in a romantic relationship. Sounds selfish, right? I also just assumed that relationships had to be hard work and that I was no good at them. How many times have you been told that you have to work hard at your relationship? How many times have you heard that you have to compromise when you are in a relationship? How well does that work? What if there was a different possibility?

Gary Douglas says there is only one thing that should be hard in a romantic relationship (wink, wink).

So, I'm guessing you are wondering about me saying I was no good at relationships because I never put myself first. Well, you might be thinking "aren't you supposed to put your partner first" or at least consider them in the decisions you make and do things that are just for them? How well has that worked for you?

Often when we start a new relationship, the other person is really attracted to us and us to them because of how *different* or unique we are. When we get into a relationship we so often cut off the parts of ourselves that have attracted the other person to us in the first place. When someone is different from us, that is often what is appealing about them and how they are unique and how they just *are* themselves. Then when we get into relationship with a person, we start doing the things the other person does and start acting in a manner that we feel that they will like or that is acceptable to the other person. We do this almost unconsciously without even thinking about it.

Oh, you like lawn bowling? Well, it's not really my thing, but I'll go along with you because it's something *you* like. Then you go with the other person and realize you were right in the first place. This is not really something that you are into doing. But you go along and participate in whatever activity it is with the other person so you feel you have a connection with them. Then after a while, the other person does something that annoys you and you think, "How could you do this to me, I went lawn bowling with you and I don't even like lawn bowling! You are such a jerk!"

So, what if, when your enjoyable other goes off to do an activity you don't like, instead of tagging along and hating it, you simply be in total allowance and tell your enjoyable other to go off and have a good time without you? Have you ever told the other person that you really don't like that activity and how about we go do this other thing that I like better? And then they resent *you*? How much fun is that?

You don't have to tag along. Do something that *you like to do instead*. Something *you* enjoy. And then, when the two of you get together again, you have both had a good time and you're not resenting the other for dragging you off to something you don't like doing. Have you noticed that when you do something you don't really want to with your partner that you are miserable while you are doing whatever it is and then you try to make them feel bad for dragging you off to whatever the activity is that you don't like? How unkind and controlling is that?

I know this concept may smack us in the face when we look at how we are brought up to be nice to others by putting their interests ahead of ours. If you really loved them, you'd do the activities that they want to do, and they should do the same for us. But really, how well does that work?

What if honouring you is the kindest thing that you can do for the other person? And, also use your awareness of what is truly required in each situation. Sometimes you will find that it *is* required for you to do things you don't necessarily want to do but you know that overall it's a contribution to the relationship as a whole. My point of view is simply that if you are *always* putting the other person's wants and needs first and never honouring yourself, it usually creates resentment. What if you were aware of what is required in each moment?

The act of you *being* who you truly *be* is generally what attracted the other person to you in the first place. If you twist yourself into all these crazy knots to try and be the person you *think* the other person wants you to be, then you no longer end up being who you truly are. Wouldn't it stand to reason that you honouring you is the kindest and most generous thing you can be for both of you?

I know that after I started honouring me more in my relationships, I have been able to create them being so much better. I have created relationships that are more of a contribution to me *and* to the other person.

How does it get any better than that?!®

CHAPTER 6

A DIFFERENT POSSIBILITY WITH WORK

Finding work that you love to do should be a really simple concept for all of us, right? Well for some people it is, but for most it's not.

I don't recall ever as a child or as a teen having a strong desire or drive to do anything specific for a career. I remember in high school feeling really stressed out the closer it came time to graduate and pick my post-secondary education courses as I didn't have a strong focus or any idea of what I wanted to do with my life.

I had the mindset that I wanted to love doing whatever it was that I was going to do for work, I just had no idea what that was.

I tossed around the idea of becoming a reporter (my step-father thought I'd be a great one because I was so inquisitive (a.k.a. nosey)). He also thought I should be become a police officer or go into the military. I actually considered both of those options. Ugh!! They would have been very poor choices for me.

I was quite frustrated when I would look at some of my friends who knew exactly what they wanted to do and how they were going to get there. Looking back I note that for many of them, things did not turn out quite as they had planned.

I went to a very small high school in a small town in mid-western Ontario, Canada. This school had less than 400 students. Our guidance counsellor's advice to me when I asked him for help in figuring out what to do for a career was, "Well what do you want to do?" In that 10 seconds I wanted to strangle him. I didn't have a freaking clue! How about helping me out?

I did an aptitude test. I scored high on being a beautician and going into the military. Really? The beautician score was laughable. I was about as far from a girly-girl as you could get.

I was an A- student and did quite well at almost anything as long as I worked at it (other than physics and chemistry so I knew that I didn't want to go into anything science related). I did very well in French but was terrified to speak in front of other people. I knew that this would be required to be either a teacher or a translator so I dismissed taking French as a major. I was very shy and completely lacked self-confidence. I also enjoyed business subjects like accounting and marketing so I ended up applying to several business programs including a five year Chartered Accountant co-op program as I figured that would at least garner me a decent paying job. I thought it was very important to get a post-secondary education that was guaranteed to create a decent income. I was accepted to all of the university programs I applied to.

Also, while I was going through one of the career catalogues I saw a write-up for a Television-Broadcasting Program. It involved training for working behind the scenes in television. I had also had a fascination with television and commercials during my teens so applied to three colleges to take that program. One of them let me in. I have no idea why. I had never volunteered at a TV station and had no background in the industry whatsoever. I gathered later on that I at least did a pretty good entrance interview and they needed a certain percentage of students from smaller communities so I fit the bill.

The big pull for me was that I thought it would lead me to a career that was totally different and exciting. The even bigger pull for me was that university was going to cost thousands of dollars and take a long time. I mean, what if I hated being an Accountant after five years of schooling? Then what? The Television-Broadcasting program was only two years and it was *a lot* cheaper. It was also specialized enough that I figured that I was guaranteed a job when I graduated. I was trying to be very practical and figure it all out with my logical mind.

I knew I was going to be footing the bill for my post-secondary education myself so I made the financially *practical* choice. College it was.

I had a really great time in College and really enjoyed the Television-Broadcasting program. I loved how creative and different it was from "normal" courses.

I also really enjoyed that I was living away from home on my own for the first time and that was very liberating. I was my own person finally and I didn't have to answer to anyone anymore. I finally had my freedom. It was party time!

After graduating from the two year Television-Broadcasting program, I got a job working at the local TV station as a Production Assistant. I worked mostly on the local news and some local sports productions. London, Ontario was home to the AA farm team for the Detroit Tigers at that time so I worked on the live broadcasts during baseball season.

After working at this TV station for two years I got laid off and moved to Toronto. There I did freelance work for a few years at

TSN (The Sports Network) and CFTO (the local Toronto CTV station (Canadian Television Network)).

Working in live TV can be very exciting and was for a time, but after a while it lost its lustre. Other than different news stories every day and different sports scores, it was a bit of a lather, rinse and repeat atmosphere. At least for me. I didn't get at the time that I needed variety. Doing the same thing day after day wasn't my cup of tea.

I thought that working in television should be exciting. Why was I bored?

This was also the time of a financial recession so doing freelance work where I was only offered a couple of shifts a week wasn't the best scenario for making a living. Then the CBC (Canadian Broadcasting Corporation) in Toronto also had huge layoffs and one of the TV networks that I did freelance work for advised they were going to be cutting all their freelancers down to about one shift a month. Yikes! I needed a reliable, steady income and to me, that meant I needed a "job."

The skills I had weren't exactly transferable to another line of work so I decided to re-train. I had enjoyed taking Grade 13 Law and there were always tons of jobs for legal assistants in the newspaper job ads so it seemed like a natural choice for me to go into that next.

I took a Legal Assistant Program at a private business college in Toronto and off I went to my first law firm. It was a very small firm with three lawyers. I recall my heart sinking into my stomach the first week I was employed there. What had I done?! I hated sitting at a desk all day working in an office and I didn't really enjoy the nature of the actual work either.

What was wrong with me that I couldn't seem to pick the right career and enjoy doing the work that I was doing?

I didn't know what else to do and it was a steady income so I stuck with it and after a few years went to another slightly larger firm in Toronto that paid better money.

After a few more years in the Toronto area, my partner and I moved back to the London area because he was getting custody of his son. We wanted to raise him in the area where he would be close to other family members and not disrupt his life any further than it already was with creating a new home situation.

I acquired a position working at a law firm in London and continue working there at the time of this writing.

You may find that rather strange after what I just told you about not loving this line of work and I guess it is. I just never really figured out what else it was that I would like to do for work.

Do I hate my job? No. Here's why. About five years ago, I transitioned into a new role at the firm where I work by using the tools of Access. Access encourages you to be in the question and to *ask* questions, without necessarily looking for the answer in your brain. The mere act of asking a question without looking for an answer brings up the energy of whatever it is that you would like to change. If we were able to sort out all of our problems using our brains, wouldn't we have done so by now? Being *in the question* is a really simple tool and it works. One of my favourite questions that Access suggests you use for anything that you would like to change is "What Else is Possible?®"

I had been working at this same law firm as a legal assistant for about 10 years around the time I discovered Access. I liked the people I worked with but I didn't actually like the work I was doing. I was bored with it and I needed a change. I started using the tools and asking questions and was asking "what else is possible?®" every day around the circumstances of my employment.

Within a very short time frame of me asking this question (I think it was a month or two but maybe it was even quicker), the HR Manager came to me and asked if I would be willing to assist with one of the other positions in the firm that dealt with working with our law students in terms of co-ordinating their assignments and their scheduling. I'd be doing this for one day a week. The person who was then in the position of Student Administrator was working four days a week and they needed someone to cover for the day she didn't work. This felt light for me so I said sure, I'd love to take it on. I didn't go into judgment that it would likely be more work for me because it felt light and I perceived that I would enjoy this task.

I started with this addition to my workload and found that I quite enjoyed it; however, I was still doing my full time duties as a legal assistant. This would have been fine if it was just covering the one day per week, but fairly quickly it turned out that I was covering more than one day a week, when the then Student Administrator had some health issues and was off frequently due to illness. I really enjoyed working with the students but did not enjoy the much longer hours I was working.

I continued to ask questions (when I remembered!) "What else is possible?®" My favourite "go to" question when I would like to change something.

Within another fairly short time frame the Student Administrator retired which meant the firm needed full-time coverage for the position I had been doing part-time.

The lawyer I had been working with approached HR and asked them to remove me from the student position as she wanted her legal assistant focusing only on her files and not on other duties. I wouldn't have liked it either if I had been in her shoes. HR let me know this and I said that that didn't work for me as I really enjoyed the new position and working with the law students. So I asked, "what else is possible?®" Well, I was told they would have to officially post the Student Administrator position within the firm but of course I could apply for it.

I applied for the position, interviewed for it and have been the Student Administrator at this same firm ever since. I still do a bit of clerking on files to fill up my role but I am so much happier and more fulfilled in this current role than I was in my previous one.

This new position is one that suits my personality a lot better and I feel a stronger sense of engagement in the work I do. I am also aware that I am more of a contribution to the people I work with than I was in my previous position and that just feels good.

By asking, "What else is possible?®" when my position wasn't working for me, I was able to create a change that was beneficial to everyone, not just to me. As a more engaged employee, I am also more of an asset to my firm and to those whom I work directly with on a daily basis.

I also realize that I have so much more ease at work overall now, even when working within tight deadlines. I used to get so stressed out and my stomach would be tied in knots and that just doesn't happen anymore.

Maintaining this job also affords me the opportunity to spend evenings and weekends seeing clients for healing and coaching sessions and teaching others what I've learned. It also provides me a bit of extra income. How does it get any better than getting paid to share what I've learned with others and helping them on their journey of expanding their lives?!

If I had my preference, would I do my healing work, writing, teaching and speaking full time? Yes. I also know that there is more that I want to add to it and I haven't quite figured out what that is just yet. I know that I am just on the cusp of something even greater and I'm looking forward to whatever that is.

I continue in this position today and I am always open to "what else is possible?®"

"We have more possibilities available in each moment than we realize." - Thich Nhat Hanh

CHAPTER 7

A DIFFERENT POSSIBILITY WITH RECEIVING

Access has taught me a lot about receiving.

When someone pays you a compliment, do you actually receive it with gratitude and with awareness and simply say thank you? If you are like a lot of people, the answer is No. Most of us, when we are paid a compliment, will almost throw it back at the person complimenting us. Think back to the last time someone said something like, "Hey you are looking good in that new outfit." Instead of gratefully giving them your best smile and saying thank you, do you say something like, "Oh this old thing? It's just something I threw on this morning."

Think about how it feels when someone gives you a really nice gift or buys you lunch and doesn't expect anything from you in return. Do you receive it gratefully and graciously or do you think, "Crap now I've got to go and get them a really nice gift or now *I* have to buy lunch next time?" Do you create an obligation in your mind where one doesn't really exist?

Try playing with the energy of giving from a different space and see what you notice. Go and do something nice for someone just because it would be fun to do and not because you want something in return.

Think about a time when you did something for someone because you wanted something in return and the "something in return" never happened. Notice how the energy of the two different scenarios differs.

Doesn't it feel wonderful and make your heart sing when you do something nice for someone just because you can and because it makes you feel good and for no other reason?

I realize I have never been very good at receiving. I know somewhere along the way I got the crazy idea that I wasn't deserving of receiving anything nice. Whether it was a compliment, a favour, a nice present, someone buying me dinner, you name it. I really had trouble receiving anything that was done for me out of true kindness.

Almost immediately after I got engaged to be married I told my mom that I didn't want any bridal showers. I thought that a shower felt like a greedy "gift grab." I never thought anyone else was greedy when they had a wedding or baby shower. I had chalked it up to not wanting to be the centre of attention, but that wasn't the real reason. Part of me was too embarrassed to have my friends and family members think enough of me to buy me and my then, soon-to-be husband presents. I had decided that I wasn't worthy of having a lovely party thrown in my honour where people brought gifts for me out of love and wanting to share in the joy of the occasion.

I had two older cousins throw a wedding shower for me and when my mom told me they were planning this shower, I got upset with her for not telling them that I didn't want any showers. She said it wasn't her place to tell them. And, she was right. It wasn't her place.

I had been brought up that good manners were very important, so I attended my wedding shower gratefully and ended up having a really good time. I know I was squirming a bit with what I thought was my lack of comfort with being the centre of attention; however, I don't think I really minded being the centre of attention. What I was truly uncomfortable with was that so many of my loving family members had spent their hard earned money on gifts for me. These were gifts that I really didn't feel I *deserved*. I hadn't done anything to *earn* these gifts. I was very gracious and thanked everyone profusely for all the lovely things I received and I know that some people had traveled long distances to celebrate my upcoming marriage with me. I was having a very small wedding so some of the women at the shower weren't even invited to the wedding.

The person I am now would have so much more comfort with having a party of any kind thrown in my honour. Okay, truth, I would squirm just a wee bit, just for old time's sake. In reality, I would have so much more true joy with it now and I would actually *receive* the kindness. How does it get any better than that?!®

A good example of my new-found receiving gene, is an occurrence during the time that I was writing this book. I had an autumn weekend when I had jammed my schedule, as usual, with lots of busyness. Most of the leaves had fallen off the trees and I knew I had not created time during my weekend when I could rake them. So, on a Friday evening in November when I got home from work, I knew that that was the only time when I had enough time to rake the leaves. So out I went around 5:30 p.m. to rake my lawn in the dark. I had thought that because we had had a day without rain and that the leaves looked nice and dry on the surface that they would be easy to rake. I was sadly mistaken in judging "my book of leave'" by their cover. Underneath the top layer of leaves they were actually quite wet, soggy and heavy. It was not the joyful, easy job that I had planned on.

So while raking my front lawn and bagging these heavier than anticipated leaves, I'm asking my angels and the universe, "Hey team, help me out here, what would it take for this to be easy?"

Well, ask and you shall receive really does work! Ten minutes later I had moved to my back yard and I was raking the leaves under the cover of my back porch flood lights. My next door neighbour lets her dog out back to do his business and she sees me raking in the dark. Less than five minutes later, she and her husband come walking over to my back gate and enter my yard. She is with rake in hand and they proceeded to help me rake and bag my leaves. I half-heartedly protested for about five seconds. They replied that they were sitting in their house doing nothing and that most of the leaves in my yard come from the trees in their yard anyway. I gratefully accepted their help and within about 20 minutes the job was done. The husband good-naturedly grumbled about the weight of the wet and heavy leaves as he carried the full leaf bags out to my curb and he tells us "girls" that we are doing too much talking while we are raking and bagging.

The "old" me would have been totally mortified that someone else was coming to help me to do *my* yard work. If I had been an insistent jerk about it and sent them on their way, which I would have likely done in the past out of sheer embarrassment that they wanted to help me, I would have been rude to them and likely hurt their feelings. And, it would have taken much longer for me to finish raking the leaves and I would have been a total cranky pants while doing the job. By receiving my neighbours' generous and kind offer of help, I had fun, I finished the work sooner than expected, and I know my neighbours felt good helping me out. I know I always feel good when *I* help someone out, especially with a physical task that involves teamwork.

When is the last time you stretched your receiving muscle?

CHAPTER 8

A DIFFERENT POSSIBILITY WITH HAVING, CREATING AND RECEIVING MONEY

My very first introduction to Access occurred when I attended a class about money that focused in large part on how we view and perceive money in this reality. The two facilitators who taught this class offered a completely different point of view.

How many different points of view did you grow up with around money?

I had always had the point of view that you had to work hard for money. I grew up believing that there wasn't enough money to go around, that money didn't grow on trees, that money was the route of all evil, and that rich people were selfish and mean. There was almost this sense of pride around being poor and never having enough. It was like a badge of honour that we had to struggle to get by.

It's what our parents tell us growing up and what their parents taught them, and so on. It's also what society tells us and it's the story that most of us buy into from a very early age so we just think that these things are true and that that is the way that life is.

There's this sort of middle class life plan that a lot of us grown up with and carry into adulthood because it's what we see in a huge percentage of western society.

You study hard in school and if you can scrape enough money together, or your mom and dad help you out, or you get a decent government loan, you go to college or university. Whenever you finish whatever level of school or training you do, you go out and get the best job you can for the best salary that you can. You work hard all your life, you try to put some money aside for retirement and then when you finally reach age 65 or whatever retirement age is for you, you get to stop working and sit around and complain about the government full time.

If you've been lucky enough to save a bit of money for your retirement and you combine that with your old age pension, maybe you get to go to Florida for the winter. And then, you die. Sounds great right? Not!

This never did sound like a whole lot of fun to me at all. I have always wanted something different. I just had no idea how to go about creating that something different.

I'm not sure I ever want to "officially" retire. I love teaching. I love seeing clients for coaching and healing sessions. I love giving motivational talks on what I've learned. I also love writing (yeah, big surprise there right?). I would stop doing things that I love doing, that are a contribution to me and to others for what reason? I can't say that I'll never slow down, but to completely stop "working", I don't foresee that for me. What I foresee is that if I discover more things that bring me joy, I'll add those to my life too.

What if creating and generating a business and extra income streams could be joyful?! You just have to find what those money generating activities are for you.

After starting to use the tools of Access and getting rid of a lot of my previous beliefs around money, my money situation started to change. I no longer have a poverty or "there's not enough to go around" mindset. This was even before I started my healing business.

The universe is an abundant place. I used to pinch every penny and never spent money on myself unless it was an absolute necessity. I treated myself as if I wasn't deserving of having and receiving nice things or experiences that cost money. I was giving the universe a clear message that I didn't believe there was enough to go around and there was definitely not enough for me. I honestly don't know where some of my former preconceived thoughts went. They clearly weren't *my* thoughts and points of view to begin with. They are simply gone and I'm grateful.

In the first couple of years after first being introduced to Access, I would receive random gifts of money from family members. I received two government rebates in one year from doing energy retrofit work on my house and other various random cheques would come in the mail for things that I had completely forgotten about.

I began to and still am receiving larger income tax returns than I did before and I've created a healing and coaching business that generates extra income that allows me to take more classes and training and do other things that I love to do.

I ask the universe to "show me the money" and although it's not always as quickly as I would like, it usually does show up in some form or another and not always the way I expect it to. Does that mean when I ask for a million dollars to be deposited into my bank account by tomorrow that it suddenly materializes? No. Do I really believe that can happen for me? Likely not. At least not yet. What would it take to change *that* point of view?

I have taught many Access Bars® and body process classes and when I ask the universe to send me students to fill my class, sometimes it will send me more students and sometimes it will show up totally different than I expect. I have had several instances where I've asked the universe for students for a class and either later that day or the next day I'll often have more people sign up for the class. Sometimes, I'll have someone contact me for a private session instead. The universe is showing me the money in a different way. I've also had times when I've thought of cancelling a class due to low numbers; however, if the energy is "light" to hold the class and I go ahead with it and often someone in that "small" class will end up being a business contact for future classes, private clients, or some other contribution to my life that I had never even considered.

I know one thing that gets sticky for a lot of people who do healing work or who are "spiritual" is that others often think that we should do this type of work for free or else it isn't "spiritual." What?! Where did that point of view come from?

I've been in classes taught by Gary Douglas and I've heard him say on radio shows and tele-calls, "Can you be more of a contribution to the planet or less, if you have lots of money?" The answer to that question is simple to me. I'd definitely be more of a contribution.

What if part of our ability to have money is about receiving? Gary Douglas' point of view is that there is no such thing as a money issue. There is only an issue with what you are willing to receive. If you don't feel that you are deserving of having money, can you actually receive and have it?

As I started to change my point of view about receiving and deserving to have money, more money started to flow into my life.

I used to be very uncomfortable receiving money from others and when I first started my healing business I wanted to give away sessions for free all the time because I felt *wrong* in asking for payment for the services I offered. I didn't value what I was offering people and therefore I was dishonouring me. Then I was reminded of the concept that, often, when we receive something for nothing, we don't actually value it, so we don't actually *receive* what is offered. We think because it isn't costing us anything, there likely isn't any value in it and we don't truly *receive* the benefit. When we are paid for our services, there is an exchange and no sense of obligation is created.

Who are we to treat ourselves with so little value to think that whatever we have to offer another isn't worth anything. What if the exchange is honouring to both parties?

Now when I receive payment from a student or a client, I look them in the eye and say thank you and mean it. I used to hurriedly tuck their payment away and never look at them. I acted as if receiving payment from them was shameful. I have realized that there's no need to be uncomfortable with receiving payment for my services. I used to want to give sessions for free and undervalue my worth.

Does this mean you should *never* give your services away for free? No. Do what works for you.

I was also asked this question by an Access facilitator which gave me a better awareness of my healing business. Is it a business or a hobby? If you have a "side business" in addition to a job you may tend to treat it as more of a hobby rather than a business. What kind of message does this give to the universe? When I started treating my business as a *business* rather than a hobby, I was able to create so much more.

My money flows have increased since I started using these tools and my ease with money is so much greater than what it ever has been before. I no longer feel like I'm *stuck* in my job. I can choose to have my job and I can choose to create more for myself and my living by having a business that contributes to me as well. By having my healing business, I also get to contribute to other people's lives as well.

This crazy thing called "Tithe to the Church of You"

One absolutely awesome, crazy way I have increased my wealth using the tools of Access is using what is called "tithe to the church of you." Here's how it works. For every dollar that comes to you, whether it's a job, your business, monetary gifts, an inheritance, whatever the source is, put 10% aside and *never* spend it. That's right, *never*. What if honouring *you* first before you pay your bills, tells the universe, "Hey Universe, I like *having* money. Send me some more of this wonderful stuff please."

You tithe to what Gary Douglas calls the "church of you." Does this sound a bit nuts to you? It sure did to me, at first. It also felt light to do it, so I started doing it and my money situation changed. If you want to try this and 10% is beyond your scope of possibilities right now, start with a smaller percentage. The point is, that you are setting it aside and you never spend it.

I have been doing this for about six years and rather than finding that I'm broke or in overdraft every payday like I used to, I now find that I have a nice sum of money set aside in my "10% account" so I never feel broke anymore. I have had to borrow from it on occasion and I write myself an IOU (IO"ME"), and I always pay it back with ease.

From Black and White to Technicolour

How does it get any better than that?®

CHAPTER 9

A DIFFERENT POSSIBILITY WITH MY BODY

I have a whole lot more ease in my body now. I actually take the time to *nurture* my body now by having my Bars run regularly, by asking my body what it wants to eat, when I remember (sometimes I listen and sometimes I don't), what it would like to wear, would it like to go to the gym on any given morning or would it like some more sleep? I know, you're probably thinking, "what do you mean, *ask* your body?"

Your knowing doesn't stop at your brain. Your body has its own *knowing* too. When was the last time you actually did something nurturing for *your* body? For years I just dragged my body around and abused it by heaping huge amounts of judgment on it. If I ate something that caused a stomach ache and I got all bloated, I would get angry with my body. What if my inner knowing and my body knew that what I ate wasn't going to be nurturing for my body? And, that doesn't necessarily mean, that I need to eat only "healthy" foods, gluten free, vegan, Paleo, whatever. Our bodies generally have foods that they do like to ingest and foods that they don't like to ingest and sometimes that can change over time or in any given moment.

I also used to be abusive to my body with exercise. I had this unrealistic fear of gaining a single pound so I would work out relentlessly and deride myself if I missed a workout. I never asked my body how it would like to move or what it would like to do when I went to the gym. I would *decide* that I had to do at least an hour of cardio to keep the fat off and lift as heavy a weights as I could handle. If I missed a workout, I'd work extra hard during my next workout and totally judge the crap out of myself for missing the workout in the first place.

If you ask your body, "hey body, how would you like to move today?", it will give you an answer in the form of an awareness. It is a muscle you may have to practice a bit, but just play with it and you'll see that it does work.

This morning I was writing my book and I asked my body, "what would you like to do today body?" A few seconds later I had the feeling, go for a walk. So I asked, "body would you like to go for a walk?" Immediately, my whole "being" was lighter. So, we went for a walk in nature and my body was humming the whole time.

Now when I'm at the gym, I'll ask my body to show me what it would like to do while I'm looking out over the equipment and my eyes will light upon whatever equipment it wants to use or I'll ask it about particular machines, weights and classes and I'll get a light sensation on what it does want to do and a heavy or "flat" sensation on what it doesn't want to do. When I listen, it's always a joyful workout. Our bodies like to move in whatever capacity is fun for each particular body.

Our bodies give us lots of messages. What if we are willing to listen to those messages? I can't say that I listen to my body all the time or even remember to check in with it and bring it along for the ride all the time but I'm a whole lot more aware of and in connection with my body than I ever used to be.

Our bodies are also very brilliant energetic radio receivers. You know that thing I talked about where most of our thoughts, feelings and emotions aren't even ours? Well, what if a lot of the physical discomforts we experience aren't ours either? Yeah, yeah, I know, this is sounding really nuts right? If we feel something in our own bodies then it's *our* feeling or sensation, right? What if it's not?

Next time you get a pain, discomfort or some strange sensation in your body and you're willing to try this, just ask the question I talked about before, "Who does this belong to?®" See if that changes anything. What have you got to lose? Except maybe some discomfort that you really weren't thrilled with in the first place. Oh, and you might have to acknowledge that this crazy stuff really does work. And, if it doesn't go away, you can ask your body, "What would it take to change this?" You may just get an "awareness" that never entered your thinking mind.

Maybe your body requires some energetic body work or alternative therapy. Maybe it requires some form of medication or traditional intervention. Your body knows what it needs.

About four years ago I had an ovarian cyst and asked several friends to run frequent Bars sessions on me to see if we could change it. I had about five or six sessions done by several friends over the course of about three weeks. When I had my follow up ultrasound, it was Bye Bye cyst!

How does it get any better than that!®

There are about 50 other energetic body processes in Access that can assist with a myriad of other issues and places where we've locked up things in our bodies.

After having received and given a lot of body work over the last 6 years, I have so much more ease in my body, and so much more awareness of what my body requires and desires from me in terms of food, sleep, movement, and touch.

I work on a computer a lot so I have had constant neck and shoulder discomfort for over 25 years. Two days into the last Access three day body class I attended, I suddenly felt all of the tension in my neck and shoulders just melt away into total ease. I had totally forgotten what that even felt like. I am so grateful for all of the Access body processes.

How did I get so lucky?

CHAPTER 10

IT'S NOT BROKEN!
A DIFFERENT POSSIBILITY
WITH SELF-JUDGMENT

Despite all the great changes I have created using the various tools, healing modalities, techniques and information of Access, I didn't actually need to be "fixed." What if we could all get that we don't need fixing. What if we could all get that there isn't *anything* wrong with us?

There is nothing wrong with you. There is nothing wrong with me. There is nothing wrong with *any* of us. But we keep judging ourselves as wrong, as less than, as something that is broken and that needs to be fixed.

If there is just one thing I would like you to get from reading this book, it would be for you to know, *really know,* that there is nothing wrong with you. *Nothing, nada, zero, zilch. Not one damn thing.* So if you think there is something about you that needs fixing, or a hundred somethings, there isn't.

We are all created perfect just as we are. Yes, YOU are perfect just as you are.

That doesn't mean that maybe there aren't some things that you would like to *change* about you, about your life and about how you be. And, that's cool if that's what you really choose. I just fervently hope that you get, "It's not broken."

I had these words, "It's not broken" spoken to me over and over by my friend and Access facilitator Sabine when I was having coaching sessions with her. She was trying to get me to get it through my thick skull that there is *nothing wrong with me*. "It's Not Broken" was her way of telling me that if I wanted to change something, then fine, let's work with that and use the tools that we have to create that change. Not from a place that I am broken and need to be fixed, but, rather from a place of "what else is possible?®" for me to use the tools of Access (or whatever else works for me) to change whatever it is that I want to change and to *play with it*. Not out of a sense of the wrongness of me but rather out of a sense of possibility and exploration and of creating something greater in my life than I ever knew was possible before.

If we keep viewing ourselves from a place of judgment, how much fun is that? Not much, right? And, how much generative change can we make in our lives if we are looking to make that change from a place of judgment?

If you can function from a place and a space that you have things that you would like to *change* in your life rather than from a place that you need to *fix* these things, how much more lightness would this add to your world?

When you look at change from the perspective that you would like to create something different that would work better for you rather than making the thing you want to change a *wrongness*, it opens the door to so many more possibilities.

What feels lighter to you? Going into judgment of yourself that you need to "fix" whatever is "wrong" with you, or making a choice to change something about yourself or your life that doesn't work for you? As soon as you go into judgment rather than asking a question like, "What would it take to change this?", you get stuck in the *wrongness* of you and it makes changing the situation so much more difficult.

What if the biggest contribution to ourselves and to the planet would be to simply get out of self-judgment once and for all?

What if you choose to become aware of every time you go into self-judgment and use one of the many tools available to stop it?

In order to create a change, you need to be aware of when you are going into self-judgment. If you aren't aware that you are doing it, then how can you stop it? And don't give yourself a hard time when you *do* go there. Just notice it and say to yourself, "nope, not going there."

How many of the negative points of you that you have about yourself have you bought from other people and picked up when they are judging themselves and they aren't even your points of view to begin with? How about asking, "Who does this belong to?®" every time you catch yourself going into self-judgment?

The more you practice, the more you catch yourself every time you go into judging you. Try putting an imaginary stop sign up in front of you or mentally hold your hand up like a traffic cop and say to yourself, "STOP!" You may want to do this silently in your head if there are other people around or they may send the men in the little white coats to come and get you.

Another really awesome Access tool to use is saying to yourself, "interesting point of view I have this point of view" for every judgment that pops into your mind.

When view things from the perspective of "interesting point of view," you get out of the judgment "point of view" of right and wrong, good and bad. This is another tool that is really so simple and so dynamic, you will be amazed at how the energy shifts if you just use it.

If you could get out of self-judgment, how much lightness would that add to your world and how much would that assist you in creating the life you'd like to have?

It puts you in a place where you can ask what would be fun and expansive for you to choose, instead of going into the right or wrong of your choices.

According to Dr. Dain Heer, "If you had no judgment of you ever again, do you know what would be happening? You would actually be choosing and creating your reality." (soundbite from Greatness of You Tele-call)

Dropping My Barriers and Being Vulnerable

I never wanted people to see me. At least not the *real* me. The me who had fears and imperfections and who wasn't totally in control and perfect. I was afraid that people would judge me and wouldn't like me. I put on the face that I thought was acceptable to the world and the face that I thought people *wanted* to see. The whole concept of dropping my barriers and being vulnerable was totally foreign to me. I would see other people who would be totally vulnerable and let others see their messy bits and I'd think, "wow, are they ever cool." I would always find that I really liked a person who was totally vulnerable, had their barriers down and were just being themselves, messy bits and all, because I realized that I wanted to *be* that. But, I was afraid.

This has been a work in progress for me. To be willing to be seen for who I really am without any thought of how people would judge me. I have been playing with dropping my barriers and being totally vulnerable and letting more and more of the *real* me shine through.

You know what? By dropping my barriers, I have created greater and deeper connections with people.

Oftentimes I have connected with people I would never have expected to associate with or people who I've known for a long time suddenly seem more interested in being around me when I "be" more of who I truly be around them. I get that me being *me* allows them the space to be themselves as well. And, some people have dropped away from me and I'm no longer a part of their lives and that's okay too. They were relating to the *me* that I was willing to show them and the me who was a chameleon for them, so they weren't actually connected to the real me anyway.

I can see that if I want something greater in my life, I have to be willing to be seen and be willing to be judged.

What if me, choosing to be seen, choosing to be vulnerable, choosing to be judged, and choosing to be who I truly be, is a contribution to others? I get that it *is* a contribution.

> *"Be who you are and say what you feel, because those who mind don't matter and those who matter don't mind."*
> - Bernard M. Baruch (also attributed to Dr. Seuss)

Some people will like you and some won't so *you* might as well be someone who *you* like.

If we all were willing to be vulnerable and dropped our barriers and stepped into being the person we truly are and let others *see* that person, would our lives fall apart or would they get better? My interesting point of view is that they would get better.

"Be yourself; everyone else is already taken." - Oscar Wilde

CHAPTER 11

CREATING DIFFERENT POSSIBILITIES WITH GRATITUDE

I have a printout of a cartoon on the wall in my office at work. It's a picture of Snoopy and Charlie Brown and they are holding hands and dancing in total glee with joyfully uplifted faces. The caption underneath the picture reads, "What if today, we were just grateful for everything?"

Every time I raise my eyes above my computer screen, I see it. It's a really great reminder and it never fails to put a smile on my face.

I know, I know, there is so much out there that has been written on gratitude you are likely thinking, do I really need to read another thing on gratitude?

If you are in judgment of yourself at all, ever, at any time, then you might just find that reading this is a contribution.

Did you know that judgment and gratitude cannot co-exist? You cannot have them both in your universe at the same time. If you have total gratitude for you *all the time*, you can't have judgment.

If you don't believe me, give it a try. What have you got to lose?

How much fun would it be to practice gratitude so that you no longer have judgment in your universe?

What if you started out your day, every day, being grateful for everything? How would that change your perspective on things? How would that change your morning, or your entire day, or your entire life?

It's been said that whatever thought pattern you start out with first thing in the morning will stick with you throughout your day. So, rather than waking up and thinking, "Oh crap, it's Monday and I have to go to work," what if you caught yourself before you started that monkey mind going? What if you thought, "I'm grateful that I have a job to go to that makes me money so I can buy food (and I like to eat)." Use whatever fits with the circumstances of your life.

Just start with *something*, anything that you are actually grateful for, even if you think you don't have that much to be grateful for. It could be the nice warm bed you slept in, or the nice warm body that slept beside you, or your kids or pets who (almost) shared the bed with you. Be grateful that you have a roof over your head, food in your fridge, a body that moves, eyes to see. Start with something, *anything* that you are grateful for and go from there. Really mean it and really feel it. Once you get this thought process going, you will be amazed at how quickly the things you are grateful for start piling up.

Dr. Robert A. Emmons of the University of California, Davis, has been called the world's leading scientific expert on gratitude. He is the author of, " *Thanks!: How Practicing Gratitude Can Make You Happier.*" He says that gratitude is more than a simplistic emotion. He finds that an "attitude of gratitude" increases happiness by 25%:

> *"While the emotion seemed simplistic even to me as I began my research, I soon discovered that gratitude is a deeper, more complex phenomenon that plays a critical role in human happiness. Gratitude is literally one of the few things that can measurably change people's lives."*

Dr. Emmons found that people who actively practice gratitude:

- Have stronger immune systems and are sick less frequently
- Exercise more and take better care of their health
- Sleep longer and feel more refreshed upon waking
- Feel more alert, alive, and awake
- Experience more joy and pleasure
- Are more optimistic
- Are more forgiving and compassionate

- Feel less loneliness and isolation.

How does it get any better than that?®

> *"Piglet noticed that even though he had a Very Small Heart, it could hold a rather large amount of Gratitude."*
> - A.A. Milne

Using Gratitude to Transform Judgment

One area of my life where I have created a huge transformation is by using gratitude and being grateful for *everything* in relation to my romantic relationships.

I was in so much judgment of me for a long time when it came to romantic relationships, especially with respect to my relationship with my ex-husband, Dann and how that relationship turned out. How could I have been so stupid to have fallen so totally head over heels in love with someone who was going to turn around and completely break my heart? I have always prided myself in being a really good judge of character and being able to read people really well. I kept asking myself how I could have missed all the things that Dann kept hidden from me. His underlying anger, his need to blame others for everything that had ever gone wrong in his life, his depression, and his underlying desire to not actually even *be here* on the planet.

It took me a long time and some really great coaching and learning some new tools and concepts and ways of looking at things for me to actually get it. There was no need to be in judgment of myself. If I were to be totally honest with myself, I *chose* my relationship with Dann with my eyes wide open to what I was choosing to see and also with the blinders on to the aspects of Dann that I chose not to see.

A year or two after Dann passed I had a coaching session with my friend and Access facilitator Juna and I said I really wanted to stop being angry at Dann. What Juna said to me was so easy and so simple and so freaking brilliant that it started to change the way I felt immediately.

She said, "be grateful for when things were good with Dann *and* be grateful for when things *changed."* She didn't say be grateful for when they got *bad* because that is still looking at the situation from a place of judgment and as long as I was coming from a place of judgment, gratitude could not exist. As soon as I went into a place of gratitude for *everything* that Dann brought to my life, and grateful for me *choosing* a relationship with him, then I found I actually could be grateful for him and have total peace with how things turned out and I could truly and freely move on with my life. My anger towards him and towards *me* for choosing him also disappeared.

And you may say, but the relationship *did get bad*, you're just sticking your head in the sand, Pollyanna! When you are angry or hate someone or are bitter, you only hurt yourself. It's only with love and gratitude that you can change how you perceive the events in your life that didn't go the way you think that you would have liked them to have gone.

How many things, people and events do you have in your past, present or even perceived future, that you are in so much judgment of that you cannot create the place of peace and ease that you would truly like to have? Try being in total gratitude for *all of it* and see what changes for you.

"It is impossible to feel grateful and depressed in the same moment." - Naomi Williams

CHAPTER 12

CH-CH-CHANGES

After using the tools and processes of Access for about a year or two (I really don't recall the exact time frame), a co-worker at my office whom I had known for about 10 years came up to me one day and said, "Hey, what's going on with you? You're different. You seem pretty happy all the time. What are you doing?" That's when I really got that *I was so much different than what I had been before.* Other people were taking notice. I really was so much happier.

The *me* I had become simply was who I had become, so I wasn't really cognitively aware of it until someone pointed it out. I wasn't the old, often grumpy me anymore. It's like when you have a really bad pain for so long and then when it goes away and you don't notice it anymore because it's gone. It's not there to "remind" you that you're in pain. My unhappiness wasn't there to remind me that I was unhappy any more.

Writing this book has been a huge eye opener for me. It has illuminated all the areas in my life that I really have changed for the better and how much easier and more fun life is now than what it was before.

Some of the changes are subtle and some of them are quite dramatic. I know that these differences have come about in large part from using the tools and information of Access and also from having my Bars run almost weekly for the last several years.

I have way less mind chatter now. I used to get angry very easily. That doesn't happen anymore and I'm much, much less reactive to previously stressful situations. I hardly ever get stressed out anymore.

I no longer have constant mind chatter. I covered this in-depth previously so I won't go into it again here.

I rarely get angry anymore and when I do, it dissipates quickly. I used to have a real issue with anger and most of it, I internalized. I don't hold onto grudges. Old hurts from my past don't have any charge on them anymore.

I have a greater sense of peace and calm now. I'm a much kinder person. Does that mean that I'm a doormat when someone tries to take advantage of me? No, it doesn't. I just don't react the way I used to, to so many things.

I am much more honouring of *me* now and I no longer dishonour myself for other people.

My self-confidence has greatly increased. I'm much more willing to be vulnerable now and drop my barriers and have people see me for who I really am.

I sleep much better than I ever used to, and my sleep was generally pretty good to begin with.

I Don't Daydream Anymore

This one is HUGE for me.

I used to spend a lot of time in my head daydreaming about what I wanted my life to look like and be like. I created a fairytale life in my head so I didn't have to deal with what my life was really like. I didn't like my life very much and didn't know how to change it so I spent a lot of time in my fantasy world from a very young age.

I don't daydream anymore. I don't actually remember the exact moment when I stopped daydreaming. It wasn't even a conscious choice where I said to myself, "that's it, no more daydreaming!" It just stopped after I'd been using the tools of Access for a while and getting my Bars run on a regular basis.

Now I am way more present and don't feel the need to go into '"wake escape dreamland" anymore as my life becomes more and more the "dream life" that I always wanted it to be.

How does it get any better than that?!®

Being in Allowance

I have so much less judgment in my universe and so much more allowance than what I used to have. Do I never go into judgment now? I would love to say I don't but that's not true. I do go into judgment a whole lot less now and I am getting so much better at not judging ME.

I have so much more allowance of me and everyone around me. I can be "interesting point of view" in so many situations now. Being "interesting point of view" was never part of my universe before.

I used to think that me judging others meant that I was aware of what others were doing and being. I was wrong. It simply meant that I was judging them because I could. Now I can be aware of what others are doing and be aware of their choices, but I don't have to be at the effect of whatever that is or think that they are wrong or bad or need to change.

Happy Body

I also don't have most of the "issues" that I used to have with my body. Like knee pain and back pain. I still have *some* things going on in my body that I'd like to change but I'm more aware now of what those things are and what tools I can use to create the change I desire.

As I noted earlier, I now communicate with my body a whole lot more. I never even knew I *could* communicate with my body before, except to swear at it when it didn't perform the way I wanted it to or when *it* got sick. I'm more aware of what it requires for food, movement, touch, and how to treat it with regard. I no longer treat it like this bag of bones that I drag along everywhere with me. Okay, at least not *all* the time. This *is* a work in progress for me.

Glossophobia

No, this fancy word is not the fear of glossy photographs. The fear of public speaking is termed glossophobia. According to various resources, about 80 percent of the population is afraid of public speaking.

I no longer have a complete terror of speaking in public. This particular change still blows my mind. I have no idea where it went, but this "fear" is gone!

I had been terrified of public speaking all of my life. When I was a kid in school, I would literally want to throw up before having to give a speech in class. When I did have to deliver a speech, I could whip through that talk in warp speed of two minutes flat (even when I'd rehearsed it in my bedroom the night before at a length of five minutes plus, just for good measure). I was a red-faced speed talking demon. Throughout my adulthood, I had done my best to avoid any situation where this particular skill was required.

After I had been using the tools of Access for a couple of years, a friend ask me if I wanted to do a talk on Access Bars with her. Naturally, given my complete dread of getting up in front of people and actually having them look at me and maybe even *see* me and hear squeaky words come out of my mouth, I said no way José right? Wrong. I said sure, I thought it would be fun and I'd love to do this talk with her. What?!!

For whatever reason, my complete terror of public speaking no longer exists. About 40 people attended this talk that I did with my friend. The small room we were booked in was packed and they had to bring in more chairs as the original set-up wasn't large enough.

Just before we started the talk I noticed that I did have butterflies, but remembered to ask an amazing question I had learned. Is this fear or is this excitement? Guess which answer I got a "light" sensation on? It was excitement! Gary Douglas shares that fear and excitement are physiologically the same so we perceive the same physical sensation whether it's fear or whether it's excitement. This is backed up by several other sources. Apparently neither the mind nor the body can tell the difference between fear and excitement. Cool, huh?

I was really looking forward to doing this talk and sharing some of the tools I had learned since coming to Access. I had a great time doing this talk with my friend, and met some lovely people that day too. Some of whom even became clients and/or students of mine.

How does it get any better than that?®

I have done several talks since and have taught numerous classes and I am always *excited* beforehand.

I have asked myself on several occasions out of curiosity, where did my fear of public speaking go? Had I simply bought other people's points of view that public speaking was terrifying and at some point released it because it wasn't *my* point of view? Had I misidentified the fear of public speaking for excitement all along and I had never really been afraid? Maybe it was both. I don't really know and it doesn't really matter. I am so grateful for the opportunities I have had to share the tools I have learned with others by doing talks either alone or in collaboration with others. This is something I definitely would not have done before Access because I would have decided that I would rather stick needles in my eye than speak in front of a bunch of scary monster human beings.

Goodbye Sadness

I used to feel really sad a lot. I don't feel that anymore so it likely wasn't mine. I also used to feel really lonely a lot and I don't feel sad anymore either. In fact, I actually enjoy having alone time. I used to judge that if I was spending time alone that no one loved me and that I was a loser and not worthy of love and companionship. Now I know that I *am* worthy.

Ongoing Changes

This journey has also shown me all the areas where I am still changing and evolving on an almost daily basis. And, I still have more things that I would like to change. Notice that I didn't say "fix?"

I feel so much more totally and completely alive and present than I have ever felt before. I don't function from autopilot nearly as often as I used to. This doesn't mean that I never slip back a bit into a snippet of the "old" me, but I never fully go back to the old me as those things that weren't a contribution to me are simply gone. I'm aware of something different now and it's a whole lot more fun to be how I am and be now.

I have so much more ease in my universe and I am way more joyful!

How does it get any better than that?!®

"You must be the change you wish to see in the world."
- Mahatma Gandhi

To contact Kim visit: kimlouisemorrison.com

For more information on Access Consciousness®
visit: www.accessconsciousness.com

From Black and White to Technicolour

Notes

Made in the USA
Charleston, SC
18 December 2015